# 1 MONTH OF
# FREE
# READING

at

## www.ForgottenBooks.com

By purchasing this book you are eligible for one month membership to ForgottenBooks.com, giving you unlimited access to our entire collection of over 1,000,000 titles via our web site and mobile apps.

To claim your free month visit: www.forgottenbooks.com/free955553

ISBN 978-0-260-54940-2
PIBN 10955553

# Foreign Crops and MARKETS

VOLUME 57                   NUMBER 13

WORLD FLAXSEED PRODUCTION (Page 244)

WORLD'S 1947-48 GRAIN EXPORTS NEAR RECORD (Page 248)

WORLD'S GRAIN EXPORT SUPPLIES LARGER IN 1948-49 (Page 250)

LATE NEWS (Page 243)

## CONTENTS

FOR RELEASE

MONDAY -

SEPTEMBER 27, 1948

*Issued by the* OFFICE OF FOREIGN AGRICULTURAL RELATIONS
UNITED STATES DEPARTMENT OF AGRICULTURE, WASHINGTON, D.C.

## LATE NEWS

Stocks of cotton in Belgium on July 31, 1948 were reported as 124,000 bales (500 lbs. gross), or the same as a year ago. These stocks represent about 3-1/2 months' supply at the current consumption rates. Consumption of cotton in Belgium for the 1947-48 season was reported at 423,000 bales, or nearly 20 percent above the prewar average and about equal to the import total for 1947-48

- - - - -

Stocks of cotton in the United Kingdom on July 31, 1948 were reported as 1,357,000 bales, a reduction of 666,000 bales from July 31, 1947. Stocks now have been reduced to about 8 months' supply, where it is expected that they will be maintained during the present season. Because of large withdrawals from existing stocks, imports declined to only 1,290,000 bales during the 1947-48 season, the lowest for many years. Consumption for the 1947-48 season was reported at 1,915,000 bales, or 14 percent above the 1946-47 season.

Stocks of cotton in France on August 1, 1948 were reported at 292,000 bales. This represents about 3 months' supply at current consumption rates, and is a reduction of nearly 300,000 bales or about 50 percent, from stocks on hand a year ago. August 1, 1948 stocks consisted of 89,000 bales of American cotton, 66,000 Egyptian, 87,000 French Colonial, and 50,000 bales of Indian. On the basis of incomplete data, imports and consumption in 1947-48 are calculated at 900,000 and 1,110,000 bales, respectively.

- - - - -

Reports have reached this office that on September 21 the Union stockyards of Winnipeg placed a temporary embargo on shipments of livestock to the Winnipeg and St. Boniface markets. Officials announced that the embargo would continue "until further notice". Livestock in transit at the time did not come under the embargo. One of the reasons given for the embargo, unofficial sources said, was the back-up at these points of cattle destined for the United States. Other reasons cited were the falling prices in the United States markets and the indifference of United States buyers in Canada to buying stock at prevailing high prices.

It was also reported that 27,000 head of cattle, including 4,000 calves, had been shipped from Manitoba to the United States, since lifting of the cattle embargo on August 16. Shipments from Manitoba have been at a rate of about 400 carloads of cattle weekly. On last Saturday (September 16), more than 2,500 head in 91 cars crossed the border.

- - - - -

Opening week wool prices at the current London auctions averaged $1.89 per pound clean basis for 64's to 70's good medium fleeces, $1.01 for 56's fine crossbred, and $.52 for 46's crossbred. Compared to prices for the closing week of the July sales, present prices are 8 cents lower for good medium fleeces but the same for the 56's and 46's.

- - - - -

(Continued on Page 259)

## WORLD FLAXSEED PRODUCTION NEAR RECORD 1/

The 1948 world flaxseed crop of 152 million bushels is the second largest on record, according to a preliminary estimate of the Office of Foreign Agricultural Relations. This year's production is exceeded only by the 1943 record of 169 million bushels and is 25 million bushels larger than in 1947. Increases are forecast for all continents except South America where indications point to a reduced harvest in the important producing countries.

The second estimate for Canada's 1948 flaxseed crop is 17.7 million bushels, 45 percent greater than a year ago, and surpasses the 1943-47 average by 65 percent. The current estimate, however, may be revised downward if rust damage in some areas of Manitoba, where acreage was almost double the 1947 plantings, turns out to be worse than first indicated.

Mexico's flaxseed production is likely to fall short of the 1.2 million bushels forecast for 1948. Acreage expansion was chiefly in the Mexicali area where production did not reach expectations and later estimates may show downward revisions.

The United States harvest of 47.3 million bushels of flaxseed in 1948 is only 5 percent less than the 1943 record and accounts for almost one-third of the total world output. This country will undoubtedly hold first place as a flaxseed producer for the second consecutive year.

A substantial increase in 1948 flaxseed production is indicated for European countries and the Soviet Union. In most of the countries there was considerable expansion in acreage, and weather conditions were generally favorable.

While the United Kingdom did not reach the 1948 goal of 150,000 acres, 86,000 were planted. A crop of 1.7 million bushels of flaxseed is expected.

The Soviet Union's flax (fiber and seed) plan of 4.7 million acres was apparently fulfilled. Production is tentatively estimated at about 22 million bushels, probably the largest outturn since prewar.

Asia's (excluding China) 1948 flaxseed output is the largest in three years and exceeds that of last year by 10 percent. India, the principal producer, harvested 14.6 million bushels compared with 13.1 million last year and an average of 18.1 million during 1935-39. Both acreage and production have declined in that country since 1940 when the war disrupted foreign trade.

Although 1948 flaxseed acreage and production have not been reported for Turkey, it is possible that the harvest equaled that of 1947 since the Government encouraged increased plantings. The 1947 crop of 707,000 bushels was more than double the 1946 outturn.

1/ Additional copies of this article may be obtained from the Office of Foreign Agricultural Relations.

FLAXSEED: Acreage, yield per acre, and production in specified areas, year of harvest, averages 1935-39, annual 1945-48 1/

| Continent and country | Harvested acreage | | | | | Yield per acre | | | | | Production | | | | |
|---|---|---|---|---|---|---|---|---|---|---|---|---|---|---|---|
| | Average 1935-39 | 1945 | 1946 | 1947 | 1948 2/ | Average 1935-39 | 1945 | 1946 | 1947 | 1948 2/ | Average 1935-39 | 1945 | 1946 | 1947 | 1948 2/ |
| | 1,000 acres | 1,000 acres | 1,000 acres | 1,000 acres | 1,000 acres | Bushels | Bushels | Bushels | Bushels | Bushels | 1,000 bushels | 1,000 bushels | 1,000 bushels | 1,000 bushels | 1,000 bushels |
| **North America** | | | | | | | | | | | | | | | |
| Canada | 307 | 1,059 | 641 | 1,571 | 1,934 | 4.9 | 7.2 | 7.6 | 7.8 | 9.2 | 1,508 | 7,593 | 6,405 | 12,241 | 17,748 |
| Mexico | 16 | 65 | 73 | 78 | 78 | 6.9 | 10.8 | 10.7 | 11.6 | - | 111 | 705 | 789 | 902 | 1,181 |
| United States | 1,451 | 3,785 | 2,432 | 4,026 | 4,518 | 7.6 | 9.1 | 9.3 | 9.9 | 10.5 | 10,991 | 34,457 | 22,585 | 39,761 | 47,391 |
| Total 3/ | 1,800 | 5,000 | 3,400 | 5,700 | 6,600 | 7.6 | 9.1 | | | | 12,700 | 43,000 | 29,800 | 53,000 | 66,300 |
| **Europe** | | | | | | | | | | | | | | | |
| Austria 4/ | 5 | 7 | 5 | 6 | | 7.1 | 5.7 | 8.4 | 7.6 | 8.3 | 36 | | 40 | 45 | |
| Belgium | 75 | 60 | 78 | 69 | 7 | 8.9 | 9.1 | 8.0 | 6.8 | | 664 | 94 | 617 | 470 | 624 |
| Bulgaria 4/ | 85 | 115 | 215 | 85 | | 6.5 | 5.4 | 5.5 | 6.1 | | 52 | 61 | 10 | 47 | |
| Czechoslovakia 4/ 5/ | 35 | 471 | 50 | 461 | 49 | 6.9 | | 5.6 | 4.0 | 16/ | 263 | | 277 | 185 | |
| Denmark | | 6 | 3 | 22 | | | | | 18.0 | | | 154 | 47 | 401 | |
| Finland 4/ 6/ | 9 | 25 | | | | 5.0 | 4.5 | 4.9 | 4.3 | | 464 | 113 | | 350 | |
| France 4/ 6/ | 92 | 93 | 81 | 81 | 82 | 10.7 | 4.7 | | | | 696 | 433 | 394 | | |
| Germany 4/ | 65 | | | | | | | | | | | | | | |
| Hungary | 28 | 5 | 8 | | | 10.3 | 9.0 | 12.3 | 14.1 | | 283 | 43 | 9 | 441 | |
| Italy | 164 | 32 | 33 | 31 | 49 | 12.6 | 5.3 | 7.6 | 11.7 | | 202 | 172 | 252 | 294 | |
| Netherlands 4/ 7/ | 42 | 23 | 33 | 33 | 44 | 13.0 | 10.5 | 10.2 | 4.0 | | 94 | 245 | 104 | 294 | |
| Poland and Danzig 7/ | 158 | 82 | 55 | 100 | | 10.0 | | 4.1 | | 16/ | 1,578 | | 561 | 600 | |
| Rumania 4/ | 42 | | 50 | 32 | 37 | | | | 2.7 | | 275 | | | | |
| Sweden | 2 | 36 | 22 | 35 | 49 | 6.5 | 2.9 | 16.7 | 16.6 | 16.2 | | 294 | 171 | 946 | 886 |
| United Kingdom 7/ | | 10 | 11 | 38 | 65 | | 20.0 | 16.7 | 20.0 | 19.5 | 52 | 784 | 360 | 760 | 1,680 |
| Yugoslavia 7/ | 33 | | | | | 1.6 | 20.0 | 9.1 | | | | 280 | 100 | | |
| Total 7/ | 650 | 650 | 590 | 660 | 800 | 5.1 | | | | | 5,300 | 4,450 | 3,600 | 4,900 | 7,000 |
| U.S.S.R. 7/ | 6,474 | | 2,656 | 3,553 | 4,730 | 5.1 | | 4.2 | 4.5 | 16/ 4.6 | 32,115 | | 11,257 | 15,230 | 22,000 |

| | | | | | | | | | | | | | | | | | |
|---|---|---|---|---|---|---|---|---|---|---|---|---|---|---|---|---|---|
| **Asia** | | | | | | | | | | | | | | | | | |
| Turkey 1/ | 48: | 37: | 55: | 70: | -: | 7.3: | 3.7: | 5.3: | 10.0: | -: | 349: | 16,096: | 139: | 296: | 707: | 14,560 |
| India 7/ 2/ | 3,885: | 3,465: | 3,334: | 3,259: | 3,338: | 4.7: | 4.5: | 4.4: | 4.2: | 4.5: | 16,096: | 15,680: | 14,580: | 13,120: | | |
| Japan 1/ | 50: | 95: | 67: | 75: | | 4.2: | 4.4: | | | | 211: | 420: | | | | |
| Total (excl. U.S.S.R and China) 3/ | 4,100: | 3,850: | 3,700: | 3,700: | 3,750: | | | | | | 19,000: | 16,690: | 15,490: | 14,500: | 14,560 |
| **South America** | | | | | | | | | | | | | | | | | |
| Argentina | 6,077: | 3,420: | 3,798: | 3,395: | | 9.5: | 11.1: | 10.7: | 9.8: | | 59,571: | 37,955: | 40,764: | 33,069: | 16,000 |
| Brazil 1/ | -: | -: | -: | -: | -: | -: | -: | -: | -: | -: | -: | -: | 79: | 1,200: | | |
| Chile 1/ | 5: | 12: | 13: | 13: | | 8.2: | 12.5: | 13.3: | 13.4: | | 37: | 151: | 170: | 168: | | |
| Uruguay 1/ 10/ | 407: | 592: | 300: | 469: | | 9.6: | 8.7: | 9.5: | 8.8: | | 3,894: | 5,159: | 2,853: | 4,087: | | |
| Total 3/ | 6,600: | 4,200: | 4,300: | 4,000: | 4,000: | | | | | | 64,200: | 44,000: | 44,500: | 38,550: | 38,000 |
| **Africa** | | | | | | | | | | | | | | | | | |
| Egypt 1/ | 7: | 7: | 4: | 11: | 22: | 12.4: | 10.9: | 12.0: | 12.7: | 14.0: | 87: | 77: | 43: | 134: | 312 |
| French Morocco 1/ | 51: | 93: | 82: | 74: | 115: | 7.1: | 1.4: | 7.4: | 5.3: | 15.9: | 362: | 134: | 238: | 398: | 1,400 |
| Total 3/ | 65: | 115: | 50: | 100: | 250: | | | | | | 500: | 240: | 320: | 600: | 2,100 |
| **Oceania** | | | | | | | | | | | | | | | | | |
| New Zealand | 1: | 10: | 12: | 80: | -: | 14.2: | 14.3: | 14.3: | | | 17:12/ | 173: | -: | -: | 212 |
| Total 3/ | 3: | 70: | 75: | 80: | 100: | | 14.3: | 14.3: | | | 24: | 200: | 200: | 250: | 250 |
| **World total (excluding China)** | 19,700: | 16,150: | 14,800: | 17,600: | 20,250: | | | | | | 133,850: | 117,600: | 105,150: | 127,100: | 151,700 |

1/ Harvests of the Northern Hemisphere countries are combined with those of the Southern Hemisphere which immediately follow; thus the crop harvested in the Northern Hemisphere countries in 1948 is combined with the Southern Hemisphere harvest which begins late in 1948 and ends early in 1949. 2/ Preliminary. 3/ Includes estimates for the above countries for which data are not available and for minor producing countries. 4/ Acreage utilized for combined plantings but excludes acreage planted for fiber production only. 5/ Average of less than 5 years. 6/ Sown area. 7/ Flax and hemp. 8/ Officially reported figures plus Indian official estimates for unreported tracts plus Indian official estimates for unreported tracts except in the years 1945-48 inclusive, when no estimates for unreported tracts were available. 10/ 1935 only. 11/ Yield calculated from seed acreage only. 12/ Includes seed from fiber flax.

Office of Foreign Agricultural Relations. Prepared or estimated on the basis of official statistics of foreign governments, reports of United States foreign service officers, results of office research, or other information. Prewar estimates for countries having changed boundaries have been adjusted to conform to present boundaries.

An official estimate for Argentina's 1948 flaxseed acreage has not been released. Plantings are believed to have been about the same as in 1947, but yields may be smaller. Trade sources report lack of moisture and damage from grasshoppers early in the season. Producers are to receive the same price for flaxseed from the current crop (30 pesos per 100 kilograms equivalent to $2.27 per bushel) as they did for the 1947 harvest.

There are as yet no official estimates for Uruguay's 1948 acreage or production. Fearing a decrease in 1948 flaxseed plantings, the Government, prior to planting time, increased the price to farmers for seed deliveries from the 1947 crop.

African flaxseed production is estimated at 2.1 million bushels in 1948 compared with 600,000 in 1947.

Expansion in 1948 flaxseed acreage was advocated by the Moroccan Government. As a result 115,000 acres were planted yielding 1.4 million bushels of seed.

Egyptian flaxseed production, estimated at 312,000 bushels, is more than double the 1947 output and almost four times the 1935-39 average.

The Algerian Government also encouraged flaxseed production in 1948. According to an official estimate 62,000 acres were planted. Large producers are given preferential treatment for the purchase of tractors, and a price of 2.7 times the price of soft wheat is guaranteed.

Although official estimates for Australia are not available, South Australia and New South Wales report 2,000 and 2,800 acres, respectively. The South Australian Minister of Agriculture guaranteed farmers 40 Australian pounds per long ton ($3.21 per bushel) for fully matured seed delivered at specified points. In 1947 growers were paid a price equal to the market price prevailing on date of delivery for imported seed of corresponding quality.

---

This is one of a series of regularly scheduled reports on world agricultural production approved by the Office of Foreign Agricultural Relations Committee on Foreign Crop and Livestock Statistics. For this report the Committee was composed of C. M. Purves, Acting Chairman, Russell S. Kifer, Regina H. Boyle, Helen Francis, Karen J. Friedmann, and Constance H. Farnworth.

## WORLD GRAIN EXPORTS NEAR RECORD LEVEL IN 1947-48

World exports of grain and grain products, exclusive of rice, during the year ended June 30, 1948, amounted to 34,612,000 long tons, nearly all of it earmarked for direct human consumption. This compares with 20,489,000 tons exported in 1946-47 and with the prewar (1934-1938) average of 28,248,000 tons. The all-time record was 40,600,000 tons in 1928-29, when exports consisted of 27,400,000 tons of bread grains and 13,200,000 tons of coarse grains.

Approximately 90 percent of the 1947-48 exports was supplied by just four countries, the United States, Canada, Argentina and Australia-- long the world's leading export surplus producers for most grains. Their surpluses were shipped to many countries around the earth, but mainly to deficit areas in Europe and the Far East, where they aided greatly in easing continued and critical food shortages. The United States alone accounted for 43.6 percent of all the grain sent into export channels during the year. Before the war, this country on the average (1934-1938) supplied only 7.4 percent of the total.

A significant feature of the trade during the year was the continued development of the postwar trend toward bilateral state trading in grains at fixed prices. Exporting countries making such arrangements included Canada, Australia, Argentina and the Union of Socialist Soviet Republics. Substantial quantities of the 1947-48 exportable surpluses of wheat in those countries already had been committed through such deals at the beginning of their shipping seasons. Of the 450 million bushels of wheat and flour exported from countries other than the United States during the year, approximately 350 million bushels, or 78 percent, moved under such arrangements. Practically all of the coarse grains exported from Argentina and the USSR also were included in this category of trade. While various types of committments, such as long-term trade agreements, bulk purchase contracts, barter deals, etc., were in effect, all were characterized by their bilateral government-to-government nature and by fixed prices or their equivalent.

Although world grain exports during 1947-48 were substantially higher than in either 1946-47 or 1945-46, the demand during the past season was much greater than during any of the preceding postwar years. In fact, in no year for which records are available was there a greater total grain deficit than in the season just ended. World import requirements for 1947-48, as stated to or estimated by the Committee on Cereals, International Emergency Food Committee, amounted to 52 million long tons, exclusive of rice. Actual world exports fell short of meeting those requirements by almost 34 percent.

Approximately 76 percent of the world's grain exports in 1947-48 consisted of bread grains, namely, wheat (including wheat flour) and rye. World exports of these amounted to 26,151,000 tons. Shipments from the United States accounted for almost 50 percent of the total. Canada, Argentina and Australia supplied most of the balance. World exports of coarse grains, namely, corn, oats, barley, and grain sorghums and millets, amounted to 8,461,000 tons, or 24 percent of all the grains exported during the year. Argentina figured as the principal source of supply for coarse grains accounting for almost 47 percent of the total. The United States accounted for more than 25 percent.

As in the two preceding postwar years, the actual destination of the world's grain exports during 1947-48 reflects the areas where the food situation was most critical. Supplies were moved to areas of the greatest need in accordance with the programming operations of the International Emergency Food Committee and its Committee on cereals. The cooperation of the various nations participating in the activities of the Committee during the past three years was an important factor in preventing serious famine in a number of countries. Of the world's total exports of 34,612,000 tons during 1947-48, European countries received 73.7 percent, Asiatic and Pacific areas 15.5 percent, Caribbean, Central and other Latin American countries 5.4 percent, African countries, 2.7 percent, and miscellaneous or other areas not specifically identified 2.7 percent.

Origin of World Exports of Grain and Grain Products
(Average 1934-1938 and annual 1946-47 and 1947-48)

| Period and origin | Bread grains | | Coarse grains | | All grains | |
|---|---|---|---|---|---|---|
| | Total | Percent | Total | Percent | Total | Percent |
| | Long tons | Long tons | Long tons | Long tons | Long tons | Long tons |
| **1934-1938** [1] | | | | | | |
| United States | 1,018,900 | 6.5 | 1,060,000 | 8.4 | 2,078,900 | 7.4 |
| Canada | 4,945,300 | 31.6 | 463,600 | 3.7 | 5,408,900 | 19.2 |
| Australia | 2,792,000 | 17.9 | 71,600 | 0.5 | 2,863,600 | 10.1 |
| Argentina | 3,560,000 | 22.8 | 7,119,300 | 56.4 | 10,679,300 | 37.8 |
| Danube Basin | 1,343,600 | 8.6 | 1,488,600 | 11.8 | 2,832,200 | 10.0 |
| Russia | 752,800 | 4.8 | 400,500 | 3.2 | 1,153,300 | 4.1 |
| All others | 1,212,400 | 7.8 | 2,019,800 | 16.0 | 3,232,200 | 11.4 |
| Total | 15,625,000 | 100.0 | 12,623,400 | 100.0 | 28,248,400 | 100.0 |
| **1946-47** [2] | | | | | | |
| United States | 10,767,000 | 52.1 | 4,136,000 | 52.9 | 14,903,000 | 52.3 |
| Canada | 6,214,300 | 30.1 | 543,000 | 6.9 | 6,757,300 | 23.7 |
| Australia | 1,314,700 | 6.4 | 51,100 | 0.6 | 1,365,800 | 4.8 |
| Argentina | 1,707,100 | 8.2 | 2,546,800 | 32.6 | 4,253,900 | 14.9 |
| All others | 662,800 | 3.2 | 546,000 | 7.0 | 1,208,800 | 4.3 |
| Total | 20,665,900 | 100.0 | 7,822,900 | 100.0 | 28,488,800 | 100.0 |
| **1947-48** [2] | | | | | | |
| United States | 12,946,000 | 49.5 | 2,135,000 | 25.2 | 15,081,000 | 43.6 |
| Canada | 5,659,000 | 21.6 | 124,000 | 1.5 | 5,783,000 | 16.7 |
| Australia | 2,777,000 | 10.6 | 373,000 | 4.4 | 3,150,000 | 9.1 |
| Argentina | 3,076,000 | 11.8 | 3,937,000 | 46.5 | 7,013,000 | 20.3 |
| All others | 1,693,000 | 6.5 | 1,892,000 | 22.4 | 3,585,000 | 10.3 |
| Total | 26,151,000 | 100.0 | 8,461,000 | 100.0 | 34,612,000 | 100.0 |

[1] From official records of the United States Department of Agriculture. Bread grain average for years ending June 30. Coarse grain average for years beginning January 1. [2] Preliminary. Exports for 12 months, July-June. From official sources and from records of the International Emergency Food Committee.

\* \* \* \* \*

COMPLETE DETAILS COVERING PREWAR AND POSTWAR GRAINS EXPORTS ARE GIVEN IN Foreign Agriculture Circular FG 8-48 which is available on request to the Office of Foreign Agricultural Relations, U. S. D. A.

WORLD'S 1948-49 GRAIN EXPORT AVAILABILITIES EXPECTED TO BE LARGER
THAN IN 1947-48

Based on present prospects, supplies of grain available for export
in surplus-producing countries during the 1948-49 year will exceed last
year's total shipments of 34.6 million long tons by at least 10 percent.
All of the increase is expected to be provided by larger supplies of
coarse grains, as the bread grain total may be slightly less than last
year. The United States is again likely to provide nearly half of the
total world trade. Increased production in Canada this year will also
result in larger supplies being available in that country than in 1947.

The extent to which world availabilities are translated into
actual exports, however, will depend upon price, procurement and other
policies and conditions in effect during the coming year in exporting
countries. This applies particularly to the U.S.S.R. and Argentina which
account for significant quantities of the total exportable supplies of
grain. The total movement will also depend upon the extent to which
balance of payment difficulties in many importing countries are successfully
met this year.

Harvesting of the small grain crops in the Northern Hemisphere is
now virtually completed. In the Southern Hemisphere, however, where the
seasons are reversed, small grains are still two or three months away
from harvest and corn is just now being planted. Only tentative estimates,
therefore, can be made at this time with respect to the world's total
supply and distribution of grain during 1948-49. This is especially true
with respect to the quantities of grain likely to move in world trade
during the current season. Nevertheless, for the first time since the
end of the war, it is possible to look forward with some degree of
optimism as far as prospective supplies of grain are concerned.

World production of both breadgrains and coarse grains in 1948 will
be substantially larger than in 1947, and will exceed the prewar (1935-39)
average. While the increase in total largely reflects a record corn
crop and unusually large wheat and oats crop in the United States,
generally favorable harvests in other areas (particularly wheat and rye
in western Europe) will provide a much better world distribution of
available supplies than was the case a year ago.

Despite the marked recovery in grain production in the main deficit
areas this year, however, several factors point to a continued need in
1948-49 for large world imports--a need that, from the standpoint of
nutrition, will not be fully met by exports of grain from the surplus
producing countries. Contributing to this need are increased populations,
the extremely low carryover of grain in many areas, the necessity in many
countries to increase consumption from the unusually low levels prevailing last year--by raising bread rations, lowering flour extraction rates
and using smaller quantities of coarse grains in the bread mix--anticipated
increases in the use of grain for industrial purposes, and a substantial
increase in the use of grain for feeding as many countries try to bring
livestock numbers up from the extreme low of recent years.

## GRAINS, GRAIN PRODUCTS AND FEEDS

CEYLON RESUMES
RICE RATIONING

The return to rice rationing in Ceylon was announced on September 3 by the Minister of Food and Cooperative Undertakings. This measure was the result of reduced imports from Burma, where civil disturbances since August have interfered with the deliveries of rice allocations to foreign countries. The basic ration is as follows (pounds per week): Adult, 2½; worker, 3; children, 2; and infants, 1½.

An increase in Ceylon's rice supplies during the first part of 1948 for the first time since the war permitted consumers to purchase unsubsidized rice above the amount of the basic rations. The August retail price of unsubsidized rice, however, amounted to approximately 9 cents per pound compared with the lower price of 5 cents a pound for rice rations. About one-fifth of all the rice sold during August was unsubsidized.

During the first half of 1948 Ceylon received slightly more than one-half of its calendar year allocations and about 45 percent of the 1948 rice to be lifted from Burma. A continued reduction in imports from Burma during 1948 may result in increased flour consumption, which was necessary when rice was difficult to obtain after the war. The rate of flour consumption in Ceylon has been declining in recent months.

CEYLON: Rice imports by country, January-June 1948,
with comparisons

| Country of origin | Average 1935-39 | 1945 | 1946 | 1947 | January-June 1947 | January-June 1948 |
|---|---|---|---|---|---|---|
| | Million pounds | Million pounds | Million pounds | Million pounds | Million pounds | Million pounds |
| British India..: | 191 | 63 | 43 | a/ | a/ | a/ |
| Burma..........: | 794 | 0 | 17 | 318 | 191 | 331 |
| Siam...........: | 202 | 0 | 0 | 0 | 0 | 0 |
| French Indochina | 23 | 0 | 0 | 0 | 0 | 0 |
| Egypt..........: | 0 | 218 | 323 | 79 | 0 | 129 |
| Brazil.........: | 0 | 101 | 183 | 177 | 158 | 19 |
| Other countries: | 8 | 19 | 2 | 15 | 14 | 0 |
| Total........: | 1,218 | 401 | 568 | 589 | 363 | 479 |

a/ Less than 500,000 pounds.

Ceylon Custom Returns.

CANADA'S LATE SOWN
GRAIN CROPS LARGER

Production of late sown grains in Canada is much larger than in
1947, according to the first official estimate of those crops.
Production of mixed grains, the most important of the late grains, is
forecast at 62.7 million bushels, compared with 34.9 million a year
ago. Corn for grain is placed at 12.9 million bushels, almost double
the 1947 crop of 6.7 million bushels, and the largest crop since 1942.
Buckwheat production, at 4.3 million bushels, in contrast, is substantially below the 1947 crop, and is the smallest harvest of that
grain in recent years.

Mixed grains are grown principally in eastern Provinces, and are
important to the livestock industry of that area. The sharp increase
in the current crop is due to better yields on an acreage about a
third larger than last year's area. Yields are reported at an average
of 40.6 bushels per acre compared with 30.4 bushels in 1947. Acreage
of corn grown for grain is also well above the 1947 level, and yields
are estimated at 51.0 bushels per acre, compared with 37.9 bushels
last year. Virtually all of the corn is grown in Ontario. The
decline in the buckwheat crop is caused entirely by reduced acreage,
with yields better than average.

Forage crops are larger than the average for 1940-44 principally
because of increases in fodder corn and alfalfa. Production of other
hay and clover is estimated to be slightly above average, though smaller
than in 1947.

AUSTRALIA REPORTS GOOD
WHEAT PROSPECTS

Latest reports indicate that prospects for Australia's 1948
wheat crop are very good in all States except Western Australia,
according to a report from the American Agricultural Attache at Sydney.
In Western Australia the condition of the crop has deteriorated
from lack of adequate rainfall. Farmers were unable to complete their
wheat seeding because of the dry conditions, and instead of the
planned increase, the acreage in that State is estimated to be about
the same as last year when 2.8 million acres were sown to wheat for
grain.

Some reduction in wheat acreage is reported in other areas,
especially in New South Wales, where the decline is estimated to be
about 20 percent. The reduction is attributed mainly to a shortage
of machinery for preparing the soil and to difficulties caused by
improperly prepared fields following last year's very late harvest.
In addition, some wheat lands on larger holdings have been shifted to
pasture, since returns from livestock and wool are as high as from
wheat, with possibly less work involved.

Shortage of harvesting machinery and spare parts is also expected
to handicap harvesting operations. Much machinery which could not be
replaced during the war years is now worn out or out of service because
of the scarcity of spare parts for repairs.

### FATS AND OILS

PHILIPPINE COPRA EXPORTS
CONTINUE DOWNWARD 1/

Philippine copra exports of 37,797 long tons in August were the smallest for any month in 1948. Total for the 8 months was 434,542 tons, 28 percent less than in the comparable months of last year. The August shipments of coconut-oil, however, were the largest since February. The total for the month was 3,095 tons of which 2,810 went to the United States Atlantic Coast. The January-August exports of coconut oil amounted to 21,685 tons, only 7 percent under the total for all of 1947. September exports of both copra and coconut oil are expected to show increases.

PHILIPPINE ISLANDS: Copra exports, August 1948 with comparisons
(Long tons)

| Country a/ | Copra distribution | | | | |
|---|---|---|---|---|---|
| | Average 1935-39 | 1947 b/ | Jan.-July 1948 b/ | August 1947 b/ | August 1948 b/ |
| United States (total) ......: | 206,801 | 585,620: | 234,050 | 51,639 | 33,094 |
| Atlantic Coast ........: | - | 116,034: | 25,860 | 7,812 | 4,261 |
| Gulf Coast ...........: | - | 77,155: | 40,398 | 5,132 | 6,746 |
| Pacific Coast .........: | - | 392,431: | 167,792 | 38,695 | 22,087 |
| Canada ....................: | - | 16,607: | 15,049 | - | - |
| Mexico ....................: | 7,260 | 1,500: | - | - | - |
| Panama Canal Zone ..........: | - | 1,009: | 1,361 | - | 403 |
| Columbia ...................: | - | 5,300: | 3,528 | 1,300 | 300 |
| Venezuela ..................: | - | 7,862: | 2,525 | 3,412 | - |
| Austria ....................: | - | 6,000: | 6,000 | - | - |
| Belgium ....................: | 10 | 10,306: | 1,000 | - | - |
| Czechoslovakia .............: | - | 7,676: | - | - | - |
| Denmark ....................: | 6,025 | 44,823: | 20,536 | 2,011 | - |
| France .....................: | 24,589 | 73,232: | 44,312 | - | - |
| Bi-Zonal Germany ...........: | 7,309 | 11,220: | 5,350 | 7,800 | - |
| Italy ......................: | 4,079 | 26,076: | 8,050 | 2,800 | 1,100 |
| Netherlands ................: | 28,415 | 7,962: | 1,800 | 1,400 | 2,900 |
| Norway .....................: | 91 | 15,719: | 4,097 | 3,000 | - |
| Poland .....................: | - | 21,762: | 20,000 | 2,000 | - |
| Sweden .....................: | 4,183 | 11,898: | 4,748 | - | - |
| Switzerland ................: | - | 12,379: | - | - | - |
| United Kingdom .............: | 80 | 24,250: | - | 4,000 | - |
| Yugoslavia .................: | - | 13,283: | - | - | - |
| India ......................: | - | 13,200: | - | - | - |
| Japan ......................: | 1,047 | 16,100: | 18,339 | - | - |
| Palestine ..................: | - | 7,510: | - | 1,260 | - |
| Egypt ......................: | 1,271 | 3,560: | - | - | - |
| French Morocco .............: | - | 6,050: | - | - | - |
| Union of South Africa ......: | - | 16,579: | - | - | - |
| Others .....................: | 8,678 | 949: | 6,000 | - | - |
| Total ...........: | 299,838 | 968,432: | 396,745 | 80,622 | 37,797 |

a/ Declared destination.    b/ Preliminary.
American Embassy, Manila.

Copra selling price c.i.f. Pacific Coast was about $245 per short ton in mid-September. Buying prices were 43 to 45 pesos per 100 kilograms ($218 to $229 per long ton) in Manila and 39 to 43 ($198 to $218) in producing areas. Coconut oil was being offered at 85 centavos per kilogram (19.28 cents per pound).

A more extensive statement may be obtained from the Office of Foreign Agricultural Relations.

## NETHERLANDS INDIES COPRA
## PROSPECTS BRIGHTER

The Netherlands Indies exported 21,948 long tons of copra in August. This brought the January-August figure to 150,614 which exceeds the total for all of 1947 by 387 tons. Shipments in September are expected to reach approximately 32,000 tons.

August output was 33,561 tons, the largest since copra production was resumed in 1946. January-August outturn was 191,574 tons compared with 110,097 in the same months of 1947. The forecast for September is 30,500 tons. Deliveries to crushers amounted to 5,019 tons in August and month-end stocks were estimated at 28,345.

NETHERLANDS INDIES: Copra exports, August 1948 with comparisons.
(Long tons)

| Country | Copra distribution. | | | | |
|---|---|---|---|---|---|
| | Average 1935-39 | 1947 a/ | Jan.-July 1948 a/ | August 1947 a/ | August 1948 a/ |
| Mexico | 12,614 | - | - | - | - |
| United States | 3,909 | 1,546 | - | - | 2,953 |
| Czechoslovakia | 4,896 | 5,000 | 2,000 | 4,268 | - |
| Denmark | 72,375 | 7,999 | - | - | - |
| France | 12,748 | 4,000 | 2,000 | - | - |
| Bi-Zonal Germany | 64,674 | - | 2,000 | - | - |
| Italy | 23,103 | - | - | - | - |
| Netherlands | 133,841 | 114,157 | 110,017 | 4,861 | 17,519 |
| Norway | 31,810 | 5,469 | - | - | 984 |
| Sweden | 6,886 | 3,200 | 5,000 | - | - |
| Switzerland | 17 | 2,082 | 2,500 | 2,083 | 492 |
| Lebanon | - | 1,525 | - | - | - |
| Singapore | 107,285 | - | - | - | - |
| Union of South Africa | - | 5,249 | - | 1,971 | - |
| Others | 33,227 | - | 5,149 | - | - |
| Total | 507,385 :b/ | 150,227:b/ | 128,666 :b/ | 13,183:b/ | 21,948 |

a/ Preliminary.
b/ Does not include unrecorded shipments to Singapore.

Copra Board, Batavia

MALAYAN PALM PRODUCTION
EXCEEDS LAST YEAR'S

Malayan palm-oil output for January-July 1948 amounted to 26,197 short tons compared with 20,003 for the corresponding period a year ago. Last year's 12-month total was 43,820 tons. Stocks at the end of July were 3,481 tons. Kernel output for the 7-month period totaled 4,780 tons, more than double the comparable figure for 1947. The 12-month production for the past year was 6,425 tons. Palm-kernel stocks as of July 31 came to 842 tons.

July palm-oil shipments of 1,578 tons were the largest since April, bringing the January-July total to 10,655 compared with the 1947 exports (12 months) of 50,771 tons. Kernel exports during July (183 tons) were the smallest since January. January-July shipments amounted to 2,839 tons. The United Kingdom continues to receive practically all the exports of palm oil and kernels.

MALAYA: Palm kernels and palm oil exports, January-July 1948 with comparisons.
(Short tons)

| Country | Palm kernels | | | Palm oil | | |
|---|---|---|---|---|---|---|
| | Average 1935-39 | 1947 | Jan.-July 1948 | Average 1935-39 | 1947 | Jan-July 1948 |
| Canada.................. | - | - | - | 9,599 | - | - |
| United States............ | - | - | - | 608 | - | - |
| Denmark................. | 226 | - | - | - | - | - |
| Germany................. | 1,410 | - | - | - | - | - |
| Italy................... | 134 | - | - | - | - | - |
| Netherlands............. | 1,304 | - | - | - | - | - |
| United Kingdom.......... | 2,115 | 5,874 | 2,839 | 23,270 | 49,764 | 10,654 |
| Other Europe............ | 2,886 | - | - | 54 | 178 | - |
| Burma.................. | - | - | - | 187 | - | 1 |
| India.................. | - | - | - | 908 | - | - |
| Borneo................. | - | - | - | 16 | - | - |
| China.................. | - | - | - | - | 67 | - |
| Japan.................. | 46 | - | - | 922 | - | - |
| Netherlands Indies...... | - | - | - | 11 | 1 | - |
| Philippine Islands...... | - | - | - | 87 | - | - |
| Siam................... | - | - | - | 293 | - | - |
| Sumatra................ | - | - | - | 8 | - | - |
| Egypt.................. | - | - | - | 251 | 279 | - |
| Mauritius.............. | - | - | - | 3 | - | - |
| Portuguese East Africa.. | - | - | - | 6 | - | - |
| Union of South Africa... | - | - | - | 97 | - | - |
| Other Africa........... | - | - | - | 3 | - | - |
| Australia.............. | - | - | - | 45 | - | - |
| New Zealand............ | - | - | - | 7 | - | - |
| British Possessions.... | - | - | - | 10,416 | 1 | - |
| Other countries........ | 11 | - | - | 569 | 481 | - |
| Total.............. | 8,132 | 5,874 | 2,839 | 47,360 | 50,771 | 10,655 |

American Consulate General, Singapore

## COTTON AND OTHER FIBER

COTTON PRICE QUOTATIONS
ON FOREIGN MARKETS

The following table shows certain cotton-price quotations on foreign markets, converted at current rates of exchange:

COTTON: Spot prices in certain foreign markets, and the U.S. gulf-port average

| Market location, kind, and quality | Date 1948 | Unit of weight | Unit of currency | Price in foreign currency | Equivalent U.S. cents per pound |
|---|---|---|---|---|---|
| Alexandria | | :Kantar | | | |
| Ashmouni, Good.........: | 9-23 | : 99.05 lbs. | :Tallari | 51.50 | 42.97 |
| Ashmouni, F.G.F........: | " | " | " | 49.00 | 40.89 |
| Karnak, Good...........: | " | " | | (not:quoted) | |
| Karnak, F.G.F..........: | " | " | " | (not:quoted) | |
| Bombay | | :Candy | | | |
| Jarila, Fine...........: | " | : 784 lbs. | :Rupee | 596.00 | 22.93 |
| Broach, Fine...........: | " | " | " | 650.00 | 25.01 |
| Kampala, East African...: | " | " | " | (not:available) | |
| Karachi | | :Maund | | | |
| 4F Punjab, S.G.,Fine....: | 9-22 | : 82.28 lbs. | " | 78.00 | 28.60 |
| 289F Sind, S.G.,Fine....: | " | " | " | 86.00 | 31.53 |
| 289F Punjba, S.G.,Fine..: | " | " | " | 100.00 | 36.64 |
| Buenos Aires | | :Metric ton | | | |
| Type B................: | 9-23 | : 2204.6 lbs. | :Peso | :a/ 3180.00 | 42.95 |
| Lima | | :Sp. quintal | | | |
| Tanguis, Type 5.........: | | : 101.4 lbs. | :Sol | | |
| Pima, Type 1............: | | " | " | | |
| Recife | | :Arroba | | | |
| Mata, Type 4...........: | 9-23 | : 33.07 lbs. | :Cruzeiro | (not:quoted) | |
| Sertao, Type 5.........: | " | " | " | 175.00 | 28.79 |
| Sao Paulo | | | | | |
| Sao Paulo, Type 5......: | " | " | " | 189.00 | 31.09 |
| Torreon | | :Sp. quintal | | | |
| Middling, 15/16"........: | " | : 101.4 lbs. | :Peso | 167.00 : | b/ |
| Houston-Galveston-New | | | | | |
| Orleans av. Mid. 15/16".: | " | :Pound | :Cent | XXXX | 31.08 |

Quotations of foreign markets reported by cable. U.S. quotations from designated spot markets.

a/ Nominal.
b/ Official exchange rate temporarily not available.

## TROPICAL PRODUCTS

INDIA'S PEPPER EXPORTS
DECLINE: PRICES ADVANCE

Exports of pepper from India for the quarter ended June 30, 1948, totaled only 3,469,000 pounds compared with 9,661,000 pounds in the corresponding quarter of 1947. Pepper exports for the first half of 1948 amounted to 9,793,000 pounds against 18,969,000 pounds during the corresponding period last year. The marked decline in exports during the second quarter 1948 is due largely to withholding of pepper stocks in anticipation of further price increases, according to the American Consul General in Madras.

Of the 3,469,000 pounds of pepper exported during the second quarter this year, 1,519,000 pounds were shipped to the Netherlands, 291,000 to Belgium, 280,000 to Italy, 112,000 to the USSR, 92,000 to the United Kingdom, 142,000 to other European countries, 710,000 to the United States, 128,000 to Canada, 95,000 to Egypt, and 100,000 pounds to Asia and Oceania.

Stocks of pepper at Indian ports and in the interior as of June 30, 1948, were estimated at about 5,000,000 pounds in the Alleppey area and 11,200,000 pounds in the Tellicherry area, compared with 11,200,000 pounds in the Alleppey area and 15,680,000 pounds in the Tellicherry area on June 30, 1947. The less favorable stock position in India this year and the reduced supply of pepper available in the Netherlands Indies have resulted in increased prices for Indian pepper. During early August the nominal price per 112 pounds of Alleppey pepper, f.o.b. Cochin, was Rs. 235/-($70.50) and Rs. 247/-($74.10) for Tellicherry pepper. It is reported that prices have advanced since August. The outlook for the next few months is for continued high prices, since pepper from the 1948-49 Indian crop (harvested from December through March)will not be available until about January 1949. No forecast is yet available concerning the size of the 1948-49 crop.

ANOTHER SMALL COFFEE CROP
FORECAST IN DOMINICAN REPUBLIC

Exportable production from the 1948-49 coffee crop in the Dominican Republic is forecast at 180,000 bags, or about the same as that from last season's below-average crop. The small outturn this season is attributed to lack of rain in July and August in the principal coffee producing sections, according to the American Embassy in Ciudad Trujillo.

Green coffee exports from the Republic from October 1, 1947 through July 31, 1948, totaled 152,346 bags (132 pounds each). Of this quantity 136,705 bags were shipped to the United States. Most of the remainder went to the Netherlands, Italy and Trieste. Port stocks of coffee as of September 1, 1948, were estimated by the trade at 20,000 bags. By October, when the new crop begins, the coffee carry-over is expected to be negligible.

LIVESTOCK AND ANIMAL PRODUCTS

ARGENTINA RELEASES CENSUS
DATA ON LIVESTOCK

The Argentine Government recently issued preliminary 1947 census
figures on the principal species of livestock. Although the 1947 figures
are not directly comparable with the 1937 data, because of the difference
in the dates of the two censuses, they do indicate substantial increases
in cattle, sheep and goats and decreases in other types of livestock
during the 10-year period. A comparison of the two censuses indicates
percentage increases in 1947 of 24.3 for cattle, 15.9 for sheep, and 6.1
for goats, and percentage decreases of 24.8 for hogs, 13.0 for horses,
38.3 for asses and 34.3 for mules. The following table gives the figures
for the two censuses.

LIVESTOCK NUMBERS IN ARGENTINA, 1947 and 1937

| Type of Livestock | 1947 Census (May 10) | 1937 Census (July 1) |
|---|---|---|
| Cattle | 41,268,470 | 33,207,287 |
| Sheep | 50,856,556 | 43,882,728 |
| Hog | 2,981,406 | 3,965,945 |
| Horse | 7,237,663 | 8,319,143 |
| Asses and Mules | 501,249 | 781,308 |
| Goat | 4,933,679 | 4,649,488 |

CUBA INCREASES CEILING PRICE
OF LIVE CATTLE AND MEATS

The beef shortage in Cuban cities and the insistence by cattlemen
for removal of price controls, recently resulted in the Government's
decision to fix a higher ceiling price on cattle and meat. The price
of cattle on the hoof was increased from the previous ceiling price of
11 cents to 13 cents per pound, and the price of beef at slaughter
houses was raised from 20 cents to 24 cents per pound. Retail prices
of meat were increased to 40 cents and 29 cents, respectively, for first
and second class meats. Prior to the increase, ceiling prices for the
two top grades were 37 and 27 cents per pound.

The Government also agreed to increase the subsidy paid to
slaughterhouse workers from 80 cents to $1.50 per processed head. Out-
look for larger beef supplies appears promising since cattlemen's
modified demands were largely met.

## LATE NEWS

(Continued from Page 243)

All meat in Spain has been reported to be unrationed for several weeks, though the prices are still controlled. This, however, is apparently a temporary situation due to unusually heavy offerings of slaughter animals, lack of refrigeration storage facilities and seasonal decline in the demand for meat. Rationing is likely to be resumed as the supply situation tightens.

— — — — —

The official price indices in France for the month of August indicated a sharp rise in both wholesale (9 percent) and retail (ten percent) food prices, according to a recent report. Meat and eggs made the sharpest increase in both wholesale and retail prices. Wholesale prices of beef, veal and mutton advanced about 30 percent and eggs 15 percent. Retail prices of beef were up 50 percent, mutton 30 percent and eggs 20 percent.

— — — — —

At the end of the first two weeks of the opening wool sales of the season in Sydney, auction prices of the best lines of free fine types showed little or no change from the opening rates which were up to 5 percent higher than prices at the close of sales in June. Broader types and burry descriptions, however, were 5 to 10 percent lower. The average price for greasy wool sold at auction in the first two weeks of the current season was 59.7 cents per pound as compared with 38.1 cents at the first series last year.

July exports of wool from Australia in July 1948 totalled 89 million pounds greasy and 13 million pounds scoured of which 11 million and one million, respectively, were shipped to the United States.

— — — — —

The United States Delegation to the Second Meeting of the International Wool Study Group scheduled to be held in London, October 4-6, 1948, will include Floyd E. Davis, United States Department of Agriculture, Rene Lutz, Department of Commerce, Donald Kennedy, Department of State and Paul Nyhus, American Embassy, London. The purpose of the Wool Study Group meeting is to exchange information and views regarding the present general wool situation, to consider any specific problems that may have arisen since the last meeting which was held March 31-April 3, 1947, and to discuss improvements in the organization and program of the Study Group.

— — — — —

According to Canadian sources, slaughter and feeding cattle exports to the United States reached 20,650 head for the week ending September 22, giving a total of 82,127 head exclusive of calves since August 16 when export control of cattle was abolished.

Lightning Source UK Ltd.
Milton Keynes UK
UKHW020219030119
334668UK00005B/112/P